Omecronon 2014 All rights reserved

ISBN 978-91-87713-02-6

Give your life to the tranquil storm

To bathe in the bliss

The tide brings

Like young children.

What if Tomorrow?

Hesitating at the gate of it all

I saw a woman weaving a seed.

Fragments of oblivion

Helped the poor lady of Shalott

Into the severed garden

Where the soil is rich

With spicy flavour

And the plant that fed us

In the first place

Weaves a pattern

Yet to be discerned ...

Oh Maya; where art thou?

The world in its prime.

The oyster is austere

In its rich taste,

The disgrace of which

Is solemn

Muteness ...

Solemn birds

      Whispering

           An anthem.

Oh Anastasia!

I scream for thee

Like the river knows

To be certain

I do

Believe in you

For yet a shallow moment.

Aspects of Rock Fire

In excelsior!
The wood turns golden.
Dawn awaits.
In solemn tranquillity,
The midnight children
Crawl to the dome
Where they dwell;
Long forgotten secrets.
Aspects of rock fire.
Red oceans part company
With the delta
And cotton soaked
By sun scorched hands
In bliss
Or other.

Flux

A Maya of motion;
A world as in flux.
It takes some precaution,
Escape from a hoax.

A matrix of notion,
To which we are drawn.
A Maya of motion;
The world makes us worn.

Our masks are like armour;
We are yet unknown.
The Maya in fervour
Will let this be shown.

A serpent now haunts us;
A problem to see.
No servant of peace; thus
No Maya to be.

A Rider of the Times?

"Is there a rider of the times?"
I asked in mute confusion.
Is there a chance for us to see
Beyond this great illusion?

All the clockworks and the chimes
Transgressed by nature's grace...
Can the bee so humbly be
In Mayan lands; no trace?

Born to Say Goodbye

Hello sunshine.

Stars unfold

A benevolent night.

I wasn't born

To say goodbye...

Stay holistic!

March untold.

A furnished sight.

I wasn't torn

Between the sacred

And the spoiled

To say goodbye...

Translucent Skies

Oh my...
To go astray
A night like this
Under translucent skies.
You are yet a baby
To my eyes
And I am but a man
Prone to do things wrong.
This is still our heyday
In the Lapis Lazuli skies
And I am but a lamb
Prone for slaughtered havens.
In my dreams I feed
On the myriad Lau.
Let this be known.

Parade of Lost and Found

Juxtaposing boulders,
Desperate as the time smears the windows;
Trying to make it big because
"big" is where the mouth is ...
Oh so hard to come by,
And oh so hard to tame,
This wind of mad fortune lost
Or won in a wonder or in between
The Sundays and the Mondays...
To touch, to win, this game;
Far too much of that old ache and pain.
I'm not to gain from its chill.

Never a mountain to climb because
Mountains are likely for adorers;
Their peaks must not be claimed
Like the tip of an iceberg would,
A cube in my drink
Or two ...

Can we make it from here?

Juggernaut vine tears down the pillows; oh

How I'm in love

With the scent of your shoulders.

A Waking World

A brittle ray of light
Sets fire to a waking world.
A gentle storm of fright
Tells tales of which we've heard.

We prayed all along for a new dawn
In ultra violet coloured spring.
The fact of it alas is torn.
Oh…memories they bring!

Let's face it; we are all alone;
Our bodies in despair.
The hardest night; we're indeed prone
To make it unaware.

The making of a waking world;
I fear it's much too late.
And history of which we've heard,
It sets our fragile fate.

No Emerald Gaze

An Indian summer.

Becoming in vain.

Where is the wine?

Hidden in the vine

Of opaque tears.

All the secret fears

We never dared

To dream of sharing.

Through heroin eyes

A child is staring.

A TV box

In two dimensions.

A crack in a mirror

Opens a horrible world ...

The child screams!

A world of tensions.

Escaping is futile;

It's in three dimensions.

Hidden in the Sun

Hidden mantras

In the sun,

Unveiled only

By a quiet storm.

A feeble voice

Fading as the newly tainted

Crawl to the damp cathedral.

Their voices unaware.

A Maya for a new season ...

Lace Game

Call the scope of colours
And Agni never fades.
A muse in a bewildered box;
A dime to time it trades.
Two powdered lips;
A lashed embrace.
A voice in trembling lace.
A sun of mint expression
Rests one moment on your face.
A shadow plays in marble yet,
The game you are to be.
With dice unthrown I call upon
The moirée you are to me.

The Fear

Transgressing clockworks;
Give me time
To shiver
Since shivering
Will cease
And I will be wiser.

Combining frameworks;
Throw a dime
To thither,
'Cause lingering
Will ease
The pain I feel despite her.

Obsessive night hurts.
Pass the wine;
My Maya,
Since Maya
Brings us peace

And makes things nicer.

Cloak of night bursts;
Hearts entwined.
It's hither.
The quivering
Release;
My Maya lessens night fear.

The Theatre and its Double

Yesterday's shadows

Unveiled ...

The spectacle continues

Out of sight;

Out of boredom.

I am as free

As the maddened stars

That play like fireflies

In the humid night sky,

Meeting your birdlike vision

With a silent nod.

Consent...

    Fragility...

        The theatre and its double.

    Where is the real?

Refined

    Flesh formation

        Ferocious friend

            Fire!

I breathe your name;
Inhale the sane.
Obscure your thought;
A mystery.
Enamoured.
The spectacle continues
Out of sight;
Out of boredom.

The stage is gone.
Your beauty still
Arouses me
And rids me of religion.
I bow as to a sacred star.

Coptic Aurore

Thy art the high air;

A desert of forests I breathe.

The blame for thee;

The shame is me...

On island storms I walk.

Alas my fears subside in vain,

The shame is all,

I am to blame.

Confuse me not

With absent wine;

Thou art my muse

A shallow time...

And years will go

In muteness still.

My breath is there;

A broken will.

I had to go

A separate thread;

To lose my way

In fear of dread.

The curse, your name!

In Arian fright;

To Coptic lands

I aim to fight.

My wisdom

In a tranquil jar

Will end this bitter

Chalk of tar.

A voice within.

I am my name,

'Til dawn appears

And rests my shame.

Aurora whispers

Names I trust.

To Coptic valley

Tears I must.

Daybreak Bloodline

A bird of prey
Ascends from a distance.
The wine is too dark
And I lose the bird.
The drink imposes
A fulfilling lourdesse
And the apple of my eye
Is 7 feet soft
In bead; breathing
Like the wine.

Lighting a moist candle scented.
I make us breakfast
And a Galette
To match the apple
Still lying there,
Unaware; I smile lightly.

Days may come

And then they go.
The calendar makes us mortal
And mortality
Will make
Our becoming ripe.

The bird of prey
Suddenly descends fast
While my thoughts
Are among the gem of my life ...
The Himalayas!
High air.
Wilderness!
Danger if I do it wrong.
Can there be a noble way
To reach the next world?

I remember
How Oxygene
Made me very weak;
Weary.

The hollow rocks ...
Sophisticated stretch.
It's a matter of boots
Or an issue
Of living or not.
There were times
When the dichotomy blurred.
Where was I?
Nowhere!
I don't exist!

In my kitchen
The lady makes
A lovely sound.
I am suddenly at hand
With a western breakfast
And Chinese pottery
With tea.
Together
We make this day shine
Like the holy virgin

In Kathmandu shines
And opens
A modest door ...
Infinity
In anticipation.
Nepal; my heart!
People are very poor
And also very humble.
Living is easy in Nepal;
And dying; a mere word.

We eat
And we are
Breathing like the tide.

The Softness

Tranquil storm.
A feather rises
And for a moment we're strangers,
Drifting away
To unknown shores
Unaware of
Any tidal wave
To bring us together
Anew.
Like babies on a shoreline
Crying for milk
Long forgotten we are
And April snow
Won't bug us
Since we're distant
Only for a tranquil time ...
Oh, you sweetness of mine!

Jaundiced Monday

Monadics thrust;

The furry clouds,

And neutral waves

Of infancy ...

The child is mine;

A game of trust.

The craving

For a sanguine dream ...

A fractal moment;

Brittle self.

I rid myself

For better health.

The impact of a chosen life.

I am unthrown

Of matter still.

The voices of the universe;

By xenon speed

They go by name.

I rest my case

In humble rooms.

The possible

Is always here.

Parable words

In mysteries.

A Sufian box.

A challenge yet.

Storm

Heavenly maidens;

A convex storm awaits.

The loneliness I hide

Belongs in shallow waters

Covered with shivering aspen leafs.

I never liked the black and white ...

I miles prefer European grey to win the fight.

Alive they sigh

A last goodbye

In vain,

For the air

That kept us warm

Is not there.

Dead children,

Born from desert wombs.

Crying I fell to the unknown.

Insanity breathing.

A tidal turn.

I am alone

Without a whisper even

To feed me.

Lions don't Corrode

A Sufian box wide open...

Hills and mountains everywhere;

An eye to catch.

There were once fairy tales

Of Lahorian talismans;

Now little remains.

Oh! High air!

My vision spreads

And from a distance

I can anticipate

A golden glow;

A border to cross

If I may.

Amritsar!

No Shallow Ship

I dived for promised lands;

Goldmines long forgotten.

A castle near a faraway beach.

I strived for waters in the sun;

Halos not outspoken.

A prayer within reach.

I now dwell in microscopic wind;

touching your gentle face

I once didn't know ...

The pines all sighed your name

In the silent kindred spirit

I once was, unknowing.

My future, you're to tame!

Oh the willowed ghost

I could have been

Without your name

To wear ...

Canvas boxer short

Of perfection, riddled mind;

World is ascending ...

Transmigration in Brackets

On a recent journey

The coffee made me calm.

I was in need

Of destinations;

Hidden hills

And valleys blooming;

In a moment

Hollow eyes,

Depicted faces,

Sounds of laughter

Transcend into...

Oh my ... Lebanese twin;

With bolts unlocked

A gate is open

With no possessions

Known to man;

A hesitation.

I can't take

Illusion at

An abstract plane.

Noise in Process Still

Noise in process still.
Asleep and yet awake.
The line is indeed blurred
Of memories that snake.

Like water from my hair;
Unfolding peace in dance.
An interim of moments;
A static form of trance.

Juxtaposing imagery
Is making up your hair.
Awake I find I'm worrying
If I was ever there.

Awake I asked a Moiran box
For guidance from the dread.
Moira got the best of me;
She laughed and said "you're dead".

Couldn't say I'm dreaming;
Wouldn't say we're through.
Could it be momentous blue
That forms a déjà-vu?

Memories of Noth

You came across like a wasted wine ...
I tried my best not to intertwine
My tears ...
Had it bad and I rid my fears.

An island got me; I took my time ...
A refugee in a sacred shrine
Of weed ...
Your voice was there
Oh, my fear to speed.

I could never believe you're true ...
You could never perceive my blue
Despair ...
In something else's care.

You lay your focus on wine and time.
I could always put blame on your cigar;
You blew smoke and I fade in tar.

An island dream.

Your desert smile.

I'm not your toy.

I should be a big boy.

No Holy Water

No holy water
In your sacred jar.
What brought you here?
Refined words of tar.

Dropping some names;
Feeding the flames.
Infant-like image
The word slowly tames.

No mermaid of love.
A silk padded world.
No gift from above;
Your lace though is curled.

No siren to me;
Your thoughts cannot be.
A silver lined pattern
Of blisters to see.

A Maya of motion;
Your silk is like dew.
My eyes from a notion,
All fall as if few.

Deceptions make traces;
Your name surely fades.
No hollow embraces
Can conjure up maids.

A world slowly turns,
The tide is for me ...
Try hard 'cause it burns,
My hand is still free.

Will memories haunt you?
Are you yet to be?
The water still rings true;
I'm asking to see.

Give me Wine, Give me Water

Give me wine, give me water

And some bread

To feel anew

As I eat

Somebody else's

Sweat and blood.

    The shoemaker!

Give me time, give me myrrh;

To bathe in innocence

Like some who dwell

In sand after the deed is done.

As the cause is lost

Let us not be forgotten,

For we crave for peace

And tranquillity

In faraway gardens

Wet with humid rain.

Summertime Gladness

Come with me to a wet season!
Cloudy skies make up
A benevolent witch.
We all know we're
Out of this world.

Permanent precision!

Born as if thrown
Into a wildfire
We call world;
The chosen one
Of last year's ordeal.

Easter for humanity!
Let 12 be 13 or 14, 15, 16 or so ...
Fed up to capacity ...
Let pi and e add up to two.
Summertime gladness

Will surely come.

Obnoxious

Travel by thought;

This train of led ...

To polar circles,

Touch all the fed

Obnoxious men; fall

Open for prey,

On feeble mint;

Obscure, a nay!

You shrug your shoulders;

Yawn your own way.

You kneel for none

Yet you feel astray.

An empty cup,

Alas I do fear,

Ancestral traumas

And a mystic tear.

A Time Being Liquid

Memories still;
An absent gaze.
Realist parallel worlds ...
The logician laughs
at infinity ...
Will we ever know?
Modalities of possibilities;
The only one present
Is a man in an alley
Asking for food.
Handing him a note
I know is not reality ...
He is at hand for me;
Of course I can't deny.

Maya; where art thou?

Are we chasing rainbows?
Are there angels

Hiding behind the silver lined clowns?
Stratic cumulus clouds
Make up a world
I know is within
As well as without.
Someone says they're distinct ...
I look at myself in a mirror
And I know that I don't exist.

There is nothing in me
But a thrownness
Into a world
Which is also
My becoming.

Am I afraid of death?

I struggle with infinity
In every single hair
On my head; my eyebrows.
I'm groomed

And yet displeased
Because of the infinite number of ways
I can appear to be
To any passing stranger
In any busy street.

Metropolis; an encore!
The daily wheel.

A light catches my attention ...
A scent; a monk.
His ironic smile
When I pose a question.
The monk is kind
And then continues his daily work
As we have parted
And there seems to be
A faint scent of incense
In my clothes.
Another trick of my mind?

Oh Maya; are you the vector raven of my metaphor dreamscape?

I light a modest candle
Only to hear the voices of ancient Pharaohs
Praising not the sun
But only the face of it.
How little did they know?
How little do we know of them?

My reveries contain a modal pyramid;
Near mint mathematical precision,
1500 years older
Than my grandfather
Who ceased to become
In my infancy.

Persia; the Greek cradle
We call democracy;
Woven in cotton
And thus protected from the barbaric world.

I was once a rider
In Persian lands.
History cannot easily
Be erased from our memories
But we try from being afraid …
Cowards we must be
In denying our past
In our daily being-to-the-world.

We seek naïve shelters
While serpents
Prey in nearby lands
And thus we are to blame
For our ignorance
In denying culture
That we once were …
The riders of Persia.
An empire in becoming!
Thus we are responsible
And what we must engage in
Is the quenching of the serpents,

Spreading with the wind
Like any forest fire would.

Not too long ago
The serpent raped
The modest path I walk
Peacefully
For we must live in peace
'Cause transgression
Is individual disaster.

A symbol we treasure
Because it speaks peace
Among other things
Was also tarnished
And poisoned for the western world to come.
I cannot wear my treasure here!
My heart craves the east
Where people are humble
And they will understand.
I am indeed one of them

And there my story begins.

Maya! I cannot breathe you here!

I must continue in becoming

And try to grow

In every step I take.

Serpents all around!

I do have something

Before I leave

To enter unknown lands.

In my mind all I see

Are explosions of a future yet to come

And I might be one

To make it happen ...

Modalities;

Possible worlds!

The one at hand

Can shift into another.

The light fades;

My eyes flicker

And I go to rest.

A German Indian ...

By tomorrow

The raven flies anew.

Au reve-oir.

A Sapphire Stare

A sapphire stare;

A severed seal.

A bond of trust ...

Alas we steal

The hours away

From humid heavens

Styled as Gnostic

Wanderers astray.

We wouldn't kneel;

We wouldn't pray ...

A novel song

To come along,

Of Mayan lands

The witch is I.

To penetrate euphoria ...

As soft archers dwell

On distant shorelines

Not forgotten.

A Shangri-La

In every hell.

The story here

Untold I fold

The blade of which

My mind's made up

And falling through

The star strewn lands

Of golden Dutch

The story of which

I'm perhaps here

To tell.

I cannot bridge

The hours together.

Masks unfold;

A dance then never

Were there any hills

And mountains

In high air.

I find a fountain;

The coin within

Was golden

Like my antidote
To Atta told and
Wonders come
As life goes on;
A severed seal.
I close the bond.
Is there no time for us?
It's in a game we're tossed?
I wouldn't like my part within
And ask for reveries
This spring;
To come of age.

Zion Fog Utopia I

Unforgettable
Like milk and oysters;
All in a blend
Within the man
Without a child
To feed
His breast from.

Unobtainable;
The cherished pastures,
Dressed in summer rain.
A starry night;
Abundant,
Like a gentle storm,
An austere dream.

Zion Fog Utopia II

The vine sighs;

A Dionysian rhyme

And infants stare

Like heroines.

An army of benevolence

Materialised

As blasphemy.

We sing and dance

A joyous rain;

Too hard to feel

The chill within

A man without

A child to feed

His breast from.

Gamma

A star implodes

From a distance

And 7000 years

Of light

Might

Do me in

When a hard rain falls

Like savage drops;

Abundant rains,

Erasing beauty.

Mute stares ...

Holy cathedrals

Crumble

To an opaque sky

The surface of which

Is you o' Baal!

"How do you do?"

Said the bat

To the elementary particle.

Autopoetry

Fractalabstractimmediate;
A time for change ...
A morning mine.

Total motions obedient;
Dada exchange ...
No time for rhyme.

All 5:th dimension compliant;
A time for laughs ...
Please throw a dime.

Which Hunt?

I couldn't conceive

The wrongness

Of an Anattanian

Twist of fate.

I couldn't believe

The untidiness

Of an Anatolian change

For heaven's sake.

Come with me

To milk and oyster lands

Made up by

A humble fire

We call lit ...

A candle sways

In desolate wind.

As of a paradox

Of will,

Then full of faith

I seek my shore.

Grandeur?

Chlorophyll communion.

Alive she cried

One August day

While spring had

Long since lost its prime ...

Avail I sigh

In times astray.

A hatter mad ...

In days; your crime

Is not to be disturbed

By absent madness

In a jar

Made up by

Musical machinery.

By Far Away

Let us go astray

This day and age

In shimmering

    Shadowplay;

        Chakras...

            Shaken,

        Unfolded,

    Like the holy Nile twists

To envision the slumbering sky

As if jaded

By oblivious

Obscurity.

Faster than the Speed of Light

A Mayan matrix;
Days of old.
It's faster
Than the speed of light.

Stars in flux;
An unknown world ...
A Mayan matrix
Every night.

Day for night;
Oh, wondrous man ...
The Mayan matrix
To discern.

Night for day;
Of Physics new.
Where are the frontiers
Yet to learn?

Our measurements refined
Of instruments to date.
Of course we can't deny;
No element of fate.

There's naturally no sense
In all of us to know
Why stars exist in harmony;
A problem yet to show.

We are aware of things
Pragmatics made us learn ...
A Mayan matrix in disguise;
A truth for which to yearn.

Twin Star

Has there got to be another me

In silk layered heaven

The space of which

Conjures up

The immaculate coldness

Of each dawn?

Twin star ...

You are my life;

My toil, my mirror.

I bathe in your distant light

And sing praise to our father.

A giant swarm...

Electromagnetic disruption.

The surface of Ur;

I will come to see

You once more

In Schwittered precision.

Heaven is Chipera

Head in the clouds;
The ice melts gently.

An extrapolating dawn ...
To trust in me;
A must you see.

A holy Grail; unfolded tree,
In chlorophyll consensus;
A reminder
Of what used to be real
And can be real,
Anew.

A barren horizon;
Some hollow knees
Kneel before
The melting I,
And for the way

I used to be I sigh
A last goodbye ...

Oh Maya; were you ever the vector raven of my metaphor Dreamscape!

www.ingramcontent.com/pod-product-compliance
Lightning Source LLC
Chambersburg PA
CBHW051702040426
42446CB00009B/1266